Creativity

ERIN MINCKLEY

BOOK SERIES BY FIG FACTOR MEDIA

WordPower Book Series

© Copyright 2021, Fig Factor Media, LLC.
All rights reserved.

All rights reserved. No portion of this book may be reproduced by mechanical, photographic or electronic process, nor may it be stored in a retrieval system, transmitted in any form or otherwise be copied for public use or private use without written permission of the copyright owner.

It is sold with the understanding that the publisher and the individual authors are not engaged in the rendering of psychological, legal, accounting or other professional advice. The content and views in each chapter are the sole expression and opinion of its author and not necessarily the views of Fig Factor Media, LLC.

For more information, contact:

Fig Factor Media, LLC | www.figfactormedia.com

Cover Design & Layout by Juan Pablo Ruiz
Printed in the United States of America

ISBN: 978-1-957058-07-8
Library of Congress Control Number: 2021923568

DEDICATION

To all of the people who told themselves "I can't even draw a stick figure" and then didn't dare to make art. This book is for you to redefine what it is to be a creator.

ACKNOWLEDGMENTS

Thank you, Jackie, for guiding me as I fly through clouds. Thank you, Nate, for encouraging me to keep being myself and never give up. Thank you, Bojana, for reminding me that life is all about dreaming and doing. Thank you, Sandy, for standing by as messy life is normalized and loving friendship is actualized. Thank you, Anwar, for reminding me to go into my imagination, away from real life, where the best content for creativity lies dormant. Thank you, Yassine, for helping me find my way when I am lost, forget something, or just need a hug to make it through the day.

INTRO

The word Creativity sums up four decades of my life on planet Earth. Every day I have been able to decide how I'm going to show up, what activities I'll participate in, how much fun I am going to have, and whether or not my wildest dreams are going to be realized. Without faith and imagination, creativity would just be play time. But, making art and designing our lives go hand in hand. What colors we paint our living rooms, what clothes we wear, the way we post captions on Instagram, or the bonds we create with friends and family—those are all choices that we make. Rules should not be applied to those decisions, because we each need to follow our hearts and care less about what other people are doing. Creativity is to sing your own song and do what sounds lovely to you. I chose to write about how I have made success in my life as an entrepreneur, artist, writer, and mother. These are the guiding principles for me, and I hope that they resonate with you.

INNOVATION HAPPENS IN STAGES

First you must imitate those who you look up to. Find someone whose work you admire. Study their style, choice of words, and tone. By emulating another artist, you learn what you are capable of. You learn that though they made it look easy, it's actually quite hard. If you are hell-bent on making something new, you might debilitate your own imagination by trying to come up with possibilities that haven't already been thought of. What a waste of time! If you fail the first time you attempt to mimic your hero: be kind to yourself. You're evolving. Innovation will arise in the subtleties of your signature style. You don't know what that is until you push through the process for a long time.

MAKING ART IS NOT FOR THE WEAK OF HEART

Writing isn't for those who like immediate gratification. Putting your ideas onto a blank paper is challenging because the gap between your imagination and physical reality will always be vast. You may take a measuring tape and try to figure out HOW far off you were, but that is useless. Try not to compare. It's like trying to put a cloud in a bottle. Instead, focus on where you can improve next time. Or just revel that you got a lot farther than people who never leave the idea stage of. At least you have something beautiful to show for your effort. At least you have something potent to start a conversation with.

ON QUITTING

You don't have to crumple your writing into a ball and play basketball with the wastebasket. You don't have to take gesso and make the canvas white again by covering up your first try. In fact, keep the first failed drawing so that you can see your progress when you hold the second attempt up next to it. Notice that the second work is easier to make. You learned in the process of making the first one, which comes in handy; you retain muscle memory in repeating the process.

CREATING BEAUTY IS IMPORTANT TO OTHERS

Those who are not "creative" gave up on their capacity to act, draw, paint, write, cook, dance, and express themselves. You are doing this work for the good of humanity. Others admire your work because they're too bashful or timid or insecure to do this work themselves. They need to live vicariously through artists to feel the rush of freedom of expression—to remind them that they are alive.

DO NOT LIMIT YOURSELF TO ONE MEDIUM

Just because you were trained as a seamstress and sew doesn't mean you can't pick up a glue stick and start putting collages together. Ignore the desire to make a business card or title for yourself that sums up everything you do. There is only one word for creator (and it's not God). It's "Artist." Art is the umbrella all creative pursuits fall under, even inventing something, starting a business, writing a screenplay, or carving a sculpture out of wood. We are not our medium. Don't feel like you have to commit to doing only one type of art. Creativity is ever evolving. Gaining mastery at one medium allows you the confidence to try a new medium and explore it with equal curiosity.

THE ONLY WAY THE MASTERS BECOME GREAT AT WHAT THEY DO IS BY SPENDING INCREDIBLE AMOUNTS OF TIME DOING IT

Do you think that the light bulb was created on the first try? No. Why would a masterpiece be created on your first attempt?

TRICKS OF THE TRADE CAN'T BE TAUGHT

You have to get good by yourself, trying again and again. Being "bad" for long enough yields getting "good." This allows you to grow in integrity. "If I can finish this, what else might I be capable of?" Constantly starting and never finishing an artwork is a great way to become disillusioned.

PLENTY OF PEOPLE IN THE WORLD ARE BETTER THAN YOU

At a lot of things. When we compare ourselves to those who are better, we discover the lack of our own capabilities. Even that hero of yours looks up to another master with the same admiration and jealousy. This should not be such a futile exercise. We shouldn't say "I quit" because we're not as well established as our heroes. Instead, we should say, "that's where I want to be" and use it as a compass. Set goals based on those you aim to be like. Let their success guide you to the success you would love to achieve.

TO CREATE IS TO BRING TO LIFE

What you make is so strongly a part of you in the moment you are making it! After it's done and you've put the pen down and signed your name in the corner, allow your work to have a life of its own. It will go out into the world and fail or succeed. It will cause conversations. It will breathe on its own without you once someone else holds it in their hands. That is magical because many people will have new interpretations of your original idea; they will add their own ideas to it. It might spur their own creation and inspire them to write or start a painting. Ideas beget ideas.

CREATING SOMETHING REQUIRES FAITH

There must be rituals or mantras you repeat in the middle of the process when you could give up. Something that reminds you: "this will work out." Remind yourself of all the times that you've wanted to give up, start over from scratch, crumple it up, toss it. Don't despair. Our minds are worse critics than most viewers or readers ever would be. Keep going with an ounce of faith that even though it hasn't turned out exactly as you wanted it to, it's still beautiful. It's perfect.

YOU CAN EASILY OVERWORK SOMETHING

Don't go past the point of "good enough." Be careful not to let perfectionism mess up a raw and vulnerable work. Sometimes we need to stop and walk away. Spend a week just looking instead of trying to solve all the problems. Face the canvas/manuscript towards the wall and ignore it for a bit. Never push the work to be done before its time. It's like trying to speed-read. You won't maintain the same level of connection or comprehension if you rush the process. There is beauty in trusting the art to tell you when she is complete.

A MUSE IS SOMETHING THAT INSPIRES US AND PUSHES US TO WORK

This divine inspiration is everywhere. In music, in travel, you will find the glorious calling to write or draw or take pictures. Let the world be your muse instead of sitting around waiting for something to inspire you. When you leave school, the world becomes your classroom. Create an assignment for yourself; begin to observe the world in slow motion. Take in beauty everywhere.

ABOUT THE AUTHOR

Erin Minckley is a Chicago-based creative. She is the author of *Artists Who Thrive* a book about resilience, relationships, and results for creative people. In 2012 Erin earned her MFA from the School of the Art Institute of Chicago. In 2016 she founded Relativity Textiles, a wallpaper brand that uses her drawings as the basis for her patterns. Infusing design with historical and cultural references, her business aims to broaden inclusivity throughout the interior design conversation. Erin paints murals and artwork in her spare time and is the single mother of two vivacious boys and one canine rascal.

www.ingramcontent.com/pod-product-compliance
Lightning Source LLC
Chambersburg PA
CBHW040002290426
43673CB00078B/340